Eleanor Mary Teresa

with best love from

Mummie.

Christmas 1948.

BRITAIN IN PICTURES
THE BRITISH PEOPLE IN PICTURES

BRITISH HORSES AND PONIES

GENERAL EDITOR
W. J. TURNER

BRITISH
HORSES AND PONIES

LADY WENTWORTH

WITH
8 PLATES IN COLOUR
AND
26 ILLUSTRATIONS IN
BLACK & WHITE

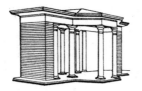

COLLINS · 14 ST. JAMES'S PLACE · LONDON
MCMXXXXIV

PRODUCED BY
ADPRINT LIMITED LONDON
———
THIRD IMPRESSION

PRINTED IN GREAT BRITAIN BY
CLARKE & SHERWELL LTD NORTHAMPTON
ON MELLOTEX BOOK PAPER MADE BY
TULLIS RUSSELL & CO LTD MARKINCH SCOTLAND

LIST OF ILLUSTRATIONS

PLATES IN COLOUR

BLACK AND WHITE ILLUSTRATIONS

THE LIVERPOOL GRAND NATIONAL, 1925
From the painting by Charles Simpson

INTRODUCTION

IT is extremely difficult to compress so important and vast a subject
as horses into a small space and still more difficult to condense it
into readable form without lapsing into telegraphic curtness of style
and dry statistics. Where my conclusions may diverge from the beaten
track usually followed by writers echoing each other without verification
especially in the matter of Thoroughbred history I must ask readers to
take for granted that I make no assertion and contradict no previously
accepted theories without the fullest investigation. Where I have hesitated
to accept as proved some scientific theories or historical assumptions
which by constant repetition are becoming rooted in the public mind and
have challenged the soundness of the premises on which they rest—when
these appear to me improbable, impossible, or in any way open to doubt—
I have set out the reasons for this hesitation and collected the facts for

7

consideration in my book *Thoroughbred Racing Stock and its Ancestry*, and in its companion volume *The Authentic Arabian Horse and his Descendants*, where full details, previously unknown and unpublished and for which there is no room here, will be found.

In reviewing British breeds we come to the final satisfactory conclusion that, whatever the system on which British breeders work, British horse and pony stock of all kinds taken as a whole is the best in the world.

HISTORICAL SUMMARY

EVERY time a different shape of ancient equine skull has been unearthed it appears to have received a fresh Latin name till we have almost as formidable an array of complications as those which gardeners have to contend with. They are increased by the fact that some of the skulls, presumed to have been those of ponies, may equally well have been those of asses or mules, so might be classed as *Equus Problematicus*! But most of this fanciful classification can be disregarded as it is often based upon nothing more than the variations of crossbreds originating from the same double source.

The original wild horse stock of the world can be divided broadly into two distinct types, Northern and Southern, and these roughly follow the human types of North and South, each varying only within the limits of its main characteristics.

THE NORTHERN TYPE. The rock pictures of Southern Europe (possibly dating from 50,000 years ago) show horse stock of the original Northern types. These cold-blooded, heavy-boned, rather asinine horses seem to have consisted of one large and a couple of small varieties, all of much the same character, with small angular sleepy eyes placed high in a convex skull with shallow jaw; they had much coarse hair, erect manes and low tail-carriage. This coarse-fibred, phlegmatic, thick-haired, thick-skinned ram-headed, slow breed with all its variations and its descendants can be classed as *Equus Frigidus;* and to it belong the prehistoric Great Horse of Europe, the big Battle Horse, our own Cart-horses, the Mongolian and the Germanic horses of the smaller type, and some of the European ponies. A large ponderous animal

NORTHERN PREHISTORIC TYPE

was also found in ancient China and Persia.

8

THOROUGHBREDS IN A LANDSCAPE
Oil painting by George Stubbs, 1724-1806

By courtesy of the Author and Messrs. Allen & Unwin

A FAMOUS ARABIAN STALLION

Seyal of the Hamdani Simrı strain by Champion Mesaoud out of Sobha by the unbeaten race-horse Wazir
Water colour by Lady Anne Blunt

THE SOUTHERN TYPE.

The hot-blooded, highly strung, light-limbed concave-headed breed, with its derivations, is native to the warm sunny climates of the south and east. Only one example of this derivation appears in European rock paintings in the form of a speckled pony; the pure Arabian only appears in the rock carvings of Arabia (where it is often depicted galloping with a rider carrying a spear) and of Egypt (1,800 B.C.)

SOUTHERN TYPE OF THE PRE-CHRISTIAN ERA

where it is shown both ridden and driven. The Arabian horse, *Equus Arabicus*, is the root stock from which all the various Southern varieties are derived. It is the source of all pure breeding and the root stock also of the racing type, being the earliest known racehorse.

The Arab tap root is the world's oldest bloodstock, passing to Europe via Egypt and North Africa and carried afar by the Arab seafaring traders long before the Christian era. Horses of Arabian origin differ radically from those of Northern type, being distinguished for slenderness, swiftness, fire, small head, tapering face, large round blazing eyes, small sharp ears, broad forehead, concave profile, thin skin, high tail carriage, silky coat and a level croup, and a different count of ribs. This breed has possessed the power (only to be found in true root stock) of impressing its type on all other breeds, since the dawn of history.

Amongst the derivatives of Southern root stock are the horses of Semitic type, desert rangers, the Indian, the later Persian and the Barb. Such varieties might be classified together perhaps as *Equus Ardens*, or "warm-blooded." Geographically, the dividing line between hot and cold horse-stock seems to have been an irregular curve bounded by the Caucasus and Himalayan ranges and the Caspian and Mediterranean seas. On and around this borderland we find, as might be expected, that the types have met and mingled, resulting in a large variety of intermediary types, many early examples of which can be studied in the sculptures of Assyria, Greece and Rome.

PONY STOCK. The prehistoric cave paintings of S. W. Europe show a much better type of pony than those found at Combarelles. They have fine, often concave heads ; the early Celtic, Icelandic and Norwegian ponies resemble this type. Leopard-speckled and parti-coloured orientally derived varieties also appear in the cave drawings of Spain. These speckled

9

ponies are mentioned in connection with Arabia in later times, and were also taken to America by the Spaniards. They are still bred in the U.S.A. under the name of Colorado Rangers and Apeloosas, and some are recorded in the American Stud Book. Ponies of this type are still found in the Himalayas. The Shetland Pony, which I name *Equus Microscopicus*, stands apart from all others as a special, more refined species, of its own ; it appears to be an original, prehistoric type.

The pony stock of the British Isles seems to be descended from the small nimble chariot ponies (seen on pre-Roman coins) which so impressed the Roman conquerors in A.D. 55. They were probably universally distributed in a semi-wild condition but the ponies of Wales, Cornwall and the Southern counties would be those which were most likely to be well bred, possibly from Arabian root-stock, as they existed in districts which had been visited by oriental traders who may have brought eastern horses to this country in very early days. However this may be, English horse and pony stock was certainly "improved" by Arabs immediately after the Roman conquest, as the Roman foreign legions brought with them horses of Arabian type. In later times the horse and pony stock in the North was probably influenced by a Scandinavian cross.

AGRICULTURAL AND HEAVY DRAUGHT BREEDS

THE CHESTNUT BREED. Goodlooking, sturdy Suffolk Punch horses are of very early origin. They have a Scandinavian, distinctly Norwegian appearance and may have originated with the Norsemen who settled in the northern counties during the ninth century ; they are the only cart breed that shows no trace whatever of Spanish ancestry : they were exported to France in the sixteenth century and known there as *Quinterots*. They were not always goodlooking, for they were referred to in the eighteenth century as "half horse, half hog," on account of their low withers and short legs ! But they were always ideal weight-pullers and plough horses for which a rather straight shoulder is an advantage. The earliest pedigree goes back to a light chestnut coaching sire called Crisp's horse of Ufford, and we are told that every animal of the present stock traces back to him.

Although, in 1872, there were still teams of bay Punches the colour now is always chestnut in every variety of shade. There are hardly any white markings except a small race and a sock, but there is often a pepper and salt mixture in the coat. Their chief points are an intelligent head with straight profile, broad forehead, large eyes : neck short, thick and heavily crested : shoulder rather straight and loaded : body deep and 'cobby' : back short with powerful, sturdy hindquarters : tail set on fairly high : legs very short, without much hair on them : action free-moving

SUFFOLK PUNCHES

but not much knee action. Longevity, vitality and good temper characterise this hardy, good-coated breed, which stands 16 to 17 hands. The Suffolk Punch has a high reputation both at home and abroad.

THE BAY BREED. Cleveland Bays are an intermediary class of light-heavy harness horse. They are largely bred in Yorkshire and are handsome coach and parade horses often used in Royal Processions. They are based on foreign heavy breeds and crossed with Spanish horses, which were the parade harness breed *par excellence* of the 17th century. The Duke of Buckingham imported numbers of these Spaniards during the reign of James I, and though no good for racing, they were extensively used to improve country-bred stock. The Cleveland Bays were crossed with thirty thoroughbred sires in the 18th century—two of these appear in all Cleveland pedigrees and were virtually Arabs, being Mr. Darley's Manica by the Darley Arabian, 1707, and Jalap, 1758, by Regulus (Godolphin Arabian) ex Red Rose by Devonshire Blacklegs.

Bay with black points, good bone, not much hair on the heels, quarters level and powerful with tail set high, good feet, and free but not high action, they stand round about 16 hands. Their heads and forehands are

CLEVELAND BAY STALLION "SULTAN"
From Sidney's *Book of the Horse.* Edition of 1892

good but they are not as a rule so well ribbed up as the heavier breeds and are inclined to length of back, so sires with this defect should be avoided as also any tendency to be "herring-gutted."

THE GREY BREED. The Percheron is the most handsome of all farm breeds and care should be taken not to depart from the true old French type. The original horse in France was a fast trotting post horse largely crossed with Arab blood during the Saracenic invasions of the eighth century. In 1755 the breed was recrossed with Danish and later with Belgian and English horses—probably an interchange took place with the latter, as the grey Shire horse of that period bore a strong resemblance to the Percheron. In 1820 two grey Arab stallions stamped the breed both as to type and colour, for though we are getting blacks now in England, this is not the right colour and is due to cheap, inferior, modern crosses of black Nivernais. This common blood also gives a goose rump which is most undesirable and has given us a wrong idea of the type. What the Darley Arabian was to the Thoroughbred, Napoleon's grey Arabian charger Gallipoli was to the Percheron and his qualities of endurance, vitality, soundness and good looks follow his grey colour. To breeders I say, "Don't lose it!"

It is from this breed that the child's dappled grey rocking horse was designed and the style is quite a realistic representation.

The real Percheron at eight years old should be a light dapple grey of striking appearance. Head small, Arab-like with very broad forehead, deep jowl, large, wide open, brilliant eyes ; ears small and delicately cut; muzzle small with very wide nostrils; arched crest and throttle ; very powerful limbs ; shoulders good ; chest broad ; quarters broad and level ; tail set on high and carried well ; feet excellent, with very little hair on heels ; good free trotting action and capable of pulling immense weights.

The Percheron is strongly pre-potent like all Arab-bred horses, and stands about 16 to 17 hands.

The Percheron Society founded in 1822 throws doubt on the oriental cross on the ground that dappled grey is not an Arab colour, in which of course they are mistaken. The cross is a matter of history.

THE GREAT HORSE AND THE WHITE LEGGED BREEDS. The Shire and Clydesdale breeds are the largest and heaviest in the world, reaching 17 to 18 hands, and the Shires weighing not less than a ton.

Both breeds represent the ancient, prehistoric Great Horse of Europe though they have been strongly influenced by the Spanish type of battle horse which had the same white legs, the blaze, the crested neck, and the profuse mane. The sixteenth century 'Courser' was expected to carry up to 32 stone for himself and his rider, and often pillion riders. As early as 1310, Edward II imported forty-two Lombardy horses and twelve horses "of extraordinary power," and during the reign of Edward III there were so many Great Horses that an Archbishop mentioned the excessive cost of their upkeep in his list of abuses, alleging that each horse cost 2/7d a week, "which would be enough to keep four or five poor people!"

Scotland also imported horses from Lombardy ; the Earl of Mar bringing fifty of these and twelve huge Hungarian mares into the country in 1553. Heavy horses were also imported from Flanders. The Shire horse of the English Midland Counties and the Scottish Clydesdale are both descended from a mixed, imported, heavy, battle-horse stock varying in type according to the country from which they came.

At the present time the colour of both breeds is chiefly bay with a blaze. The Clydesdales being particularly distinguished for four white stockings and sometimes a white patch on the belly inherited from the black Flemish stallion of Lochlyoch in 1715, whose progeny were mostly black or brown with these markings. The breeds have been crossed and the Shire, which has rather less white markings and shows signs of more ordinary cart blood, is less magnificent in appearance than the Clydesdale which is more particularly the product of Scotland and is less generally distributed throughout this country than the Shire. The prices of these horses may reach up to 1,000 guineas for show winners.

"Lynford Viking,"
Lord Brocket's Champion Percheron Stallion

The Shire is even larger than the Clydesdale and does not show quite so much quality, his breeding having been neglected during the first half of the nineteenth century. The breed, however, was in existence under the same name in the time of Henry VIII, all horses bred in the Shires being loosely termed Shires. Grey was the original colour and is gradually returning to favour, though bay is more usual and is probably the result of Clydesdale admixture : I cannot trace the alleged connection with the Fen black horse imported by William III. Fifty years ago there were very fine teams of piebalds. The Clydesdale's points are a small head in proportion to the body but still of massive beauty and carried proudly ; slightly convex profile tapering towards muzzle ; ears small and well cut ; eyes rather large and intelligent ; neck finely crested ; shoulders good ; very powerful back, quarters, loins, thighs and hocks ; tail set rather high ; feet sound and strong, their hard wearing capacity being of great importance ; action smart and good. The horse is very active for his size and is undoubtedly the world's finest agricultural type of the heaviest class. The Shire's points are a heavy convex head ; short neck ; short and straight back ; wide quarters ; tail set rather low ; legs very powerful with 11 inches of bone under the knee and 12 under the hock ; much hair on the legs ; feet open and wide at heels ; action rather slow and ponderous.

THE FARM HORSE OF MIXED BREED.   Strong farm horses of mixed breed have been extremely useful to British farmers ever since the day when they first began to replace oxen at the plough.   At the beginning of the twelfth century they were yoked with the oxen, being sometimes driven together in teams of sixteen and twenty, and by the end of that century they were in use for ploughs, sledges and carts.   A hundred years later the value of a "cart" horse had risen from 6s. to 18s.   The smaller packhorse and farm animals (rounceys, stotts, etc.) had fetched from 3s. to 11/8d. in the preceding period.   Berkshire farmers drove teams of six stallions; in Sussex, bells adorned the harness which were to warn people coming along the narrow corkscrew lanes of the weald.

In 1651 carthorses were a mixture of Germanic breeds, mostly dun and white, and crossed with Belgian, Italian, Spanish and Barb or Arab blood.   In 1680 William III imported a large black breed of Dutch cart-horses which are erroneously now referred to as the "Old English Black Horse" of Fen breed, and often said to be the origin of the Shire, but the Shire was already known in the time of Henry VIII, and the Shire horses of the Fens were not black but parti-coloured chestnut and grey; the black horses were also known as the "snail breed" on account of their slowness.

At the end of the eighteenth century, Bakewell of Dishley—a celebrated sheep and cattle breeder—set about improving it by intensive inbreeding

TEAM OF CLYDESDALES

15

SHIRE AND SHETLAND
From Sidney's *Book of the Horse*. Edition of 1892

to horses whose breeding he kept a close secret. By a process of three
new blades and two new handles he got rid of the long thick hairy legs
described by Defoe but in 1788 Marshall, who had praised one of Bakewell's stallions four years earlier still wrote lamenting the disastrous
infiltration of the "Howden muck" into the Vale of Pickering condemning
the whole breed as a plague, adding "The breed of grey rats with which
this Island has of late been overrun is not a greater pest than this breed of
black Fen horses." Proverbially slow and ugly they were very powerful,
the largest reaching 18 hands and able to draw three tons ; but it is perhaps
not surprising that either Bakewell entirely transformed them by crossing,
or the type died out with the vast influx of later importations.

In the agricultural horses of to-day we have, on the one hand, these
special breeds—Shires, Clydesdales, the Suffolk Punch, the Cleveland Bay
and so on, and on the other, the still varied collection of farmhorses of
mixed breed, and allied types, all useful horses of recognisable general type.

Farm horses may therefore have Shire or Percheron or any other heavy
blood in them and all are of mixed origin. A similar mixed origin is
responsible for the lighter van horses and tradesmen's ponies, for not only
leading sires of the best heavy breeds, but also many Thoroughbred,

BARB HORSE
Water colour by Lady Anne Blunt, 1872

Hackney, Hunter and pony stallions have travelled the country for years and have modified all stock to a certain extent, producing heavy hunter types, light hacks, polo ponies, etc., according to what mares were brought to them by farmers.

RACING STRAINS

THE MODERN THOROUGHBRED RACEHORSE. The English Thoroughbred, though foreign by blood, is called 'English' because of the long time it has been bred and developed in England and 'Thoroughbred' because it originated from the Arabic 'Kehilan' of which 'Thoroughbred' is the literal translation and which is the generic term for the Arabian breed meaning "pure bred all through." It was first translated 'Bred horses' for Arabians bred in England. The word 'Natural ' was sometimes used to distinguish those actually foaled in Arabia or Barbary, but a confusion arose between Barbs, Arabs and Turks owing to Arabians being imported via North Africa and Turkey (which then included Irak and part of N. Arabia) or from the Arab Studs of Oriental potentates, notably of Morocco, who prided themselves on the Arab strains kept pure since the Saracen conquest. Leo Africanus, writing in the seventeenth century, also pointed out the mistake by which the Arab of Arabia was miscalled Barb because "Barbarian" was a word used as we now use "foreign" and was confused with the Barbary States. A Barbary horse merely meant a foreign horse from "outlandish" countries. Contrary to Ridgway's Libyan theory there were no Barb horses or horses of any kind in Libya or the Barbary States prehistorically, and the later horses of N. Africa were a cosmopolitan mixture of hot and cold blood with the Spanish ram's head and drooping quarters, excellent working horses and much favoured, like Spanish horses, for High School. They only gained a reputation for excellence and a turn of speed after the Saracen invasion when Arab tribes settled in Barbary and Morocco with their horses and improved the local stock which was good in proportion to the amount of Arab blood in it. Native Barbs were not considered at any time as fast or as valuable as Arabs, their relative prices in the seventeenth century being £25 to £3000. Since then they have been crossed with thoroughbred and cart horse blood from England to give size but they have always continued inferior to Arabs in speed, the latter being reckoned able to give them a stone.

The intermixture of slower blood may well be represented by the blanks in the pedigree which have recently been absurdly assumed to represent some wonderful native racing mares. I cannot emphasize too strongly that where a foundation mare is "unknown" this does not imply that she was English by blood. There was not a single non-oriental racing sire, and there is not the smallest evidence of any such breed of females and, as it is pretty obvious that there is common blood somewhere, it is probable that real blanks so far from being racehorses represent the flaws of common blood, every drop of which acts as a clog on speed and of which we are still trying to rid ourselves. There may have been small pony blood as racing was originally for 12 and 13 hands, but this again would not be a dominating factor and was pretty well wiped out by Henry VIII. It is also important to remember that 'Coursers' (another misleading word) were not racehorses but huge war horses. In the time of heavy armour weighing 32 stone plus the rider, nothing less powerful than a Mecklenburg half-bred cart horse could carry the weight. These enormous animals were not expected to move beyond a walk except for about a hundred yards in a "course" or charge at a tournament or tilting match. A courser was therefore another word for a charger, though later it was used of a horse for coursing hares and eventually for a racehorse.

In 1644, General Lord Fairfax in a lengthy treatise made it quite clear that all breeds large and small were foreign importations, such native horses as might be called English being of a slow common kind and even these had continental blood. Being essentially a Cavalry man and judging horses by avoirdupois weight like Henry VIII, he extols the large foreign

DARLEY ARABIAN
Aquatint by J. Sartorius, Senior, c. 1685

heavy breed for war and deplores the recent craze for oriental racehorses as not comparable to the powerful armour carriers and calls them "over-valued pigmy baubles" only useful for the despicable pleasure of racing and no good for heavy armour; yet even he cannot resist advising a cross of Barbary to warm up the phlegmatic local stock. It really was not surprising that the non-military horsemen should have got tired of this perpetual influx of carthorses due to the influence of Henry VIII and the heavy armour of the time and turned to the Arab, whose racing reputation was already established as early as 1,300 B.C.

In the fifteenth century racing was in full swing in Egypt. Huge prices comparable to those now given for our best blood stock were paid for Arab racehorses, topped by Sultan el Naseri's purchase of the El Karta filly for the world's record price of 64,000 Turkish pounds (equivalent to guineas). There was nothing at that time to touch the pure Arabian for speed. The only British horses which escaped the massacre of those under 15 hands ordered by Henry VIII were probably the wild mountain and moorland ponies far away in Wales and Scotland or in the Forests of the Southern Counties. The Arab racers Arundel and Truncefice were the first recorded racehorses in Britain in 1377. Arundel was sold for

£20,000 and no doubt his reputation had lingered on. When plate armour was replaced by light armour the craze for colossal horses abated and James I collected a racing stud at Tutbury headed by one of Mr. Markham's Arabians, much praised by Markham and disparaged by the High School enthusiast, the Duke of Newcastle, whose beau-ideal of a perfect horse varied according to the number of successive springs it could give into the air, without dying of heart disease ! The Stud was full of this Arabian progeny till it was sold and disappeared on the death of Charles I. It is to Cromwell we owe the reconstruction of horse breeding by imported Arabs followed on vigorously by that lover of beauty and refinement, Charles II, who seized Cromwell's Stud within an hour of his return to England and after a vain search for the Tutbury horses despatched numberless agents to buy horses and mares and spent colossal sums yearly importing them. It was the Arab mares brought from the Levant, the tradition of whose purchase still lingers in Arabia, which were termed and known ever after as Royal Mares together with their progeny. They appear in the Oriental section of the G.S.B. and also in the still earlier records of John Cheny, 1727.

All thoroughbreds trace back in the male line to three Arabian Sires : The Darley Arabian, the Godolphin Arabian and the Byerley Turk (so called) whose picture also shows an Arabian. But other sires not in the direct male top line of descent exercise a still greater influence on pedigrees taken in bulk, namely the Leedes Arabian and the two Darcy "Turks" and an Arabian un-named in the G.S.B. but which appears in the Milbanke collection of pictures as "Sultan."

The Darley Arabian is the best known to the public and dominates almost all pedigrees. The Godolphin Arabian, entered in Lord Godolphin's Stud Book as an Arabian and correctly entered as such in the G.S.B has recently been claimed as a Barb on the strength of a badly drawn head in a posthumous picture of no historic value whatever. The one genuine picture of the horse at the age of seven was painted and signed by Wootton and shows him to be an undoubted Arabian with no trace whatever of a Barb head. He was of the Jilfan strain. The Byerley "Turk" (wrongly spelt Byerly) also ranks high in the male line and was an Arab Cavalry Charger but the Leedes Arabian eclipses these two in pedigrees taken in bulk. A great confusion has been caused by imported horses going by several different names with changes of ownership and having the name of successive places and countries tacked on to them.

Every thoroughbred also traces back to a mere handful of tap root foundation mares classified by an Australian, Bruce Lowe, into 43 families ; but he did not go far enough. I have worked out these families again and find that some of the numbers can be traced back to others already numbered so that the winners attributed to subsequent families are therefore merged into previous ones and are reduced to 18, the other 7 being

GODOLPHIN ARABIAN
Engraving by S. Mackrell after F. C. Turner

unimportant. To one or other of these 18 foundation mares all our winners trace back in direct female line, but the foundation mares which influence the pedigrees when taken in bulk far outweigh any possible influence the direct female tap root may exercise unless she is also similarly repeated, just as the Darcy Turks and the unnamed Arabian completely swamp all three of the direct male line sires.

An Arabian mare called Old Bald Peg No. 6 has exercised a saturating influence far greater than that of any of the sires. Again the Alcock Arabian is a dominating influence; he is the ancestor of all greys now existing, the colour having persisted in unbroken descent for 240 years.

I have compiled a dictionary from which it is possible to work out the proportion of bulk figures of 10 tap roots in the pedigree of any registered Thoroughbred as in the following Table. It must be remembered that in a pedigree of 26 generations it represents 134, 217, 726 units against 26 units of the top or bottom line taken singly. The bulk therefore counts more than the direct male and female descent.

Name of Winner	Godolphin Arabian	Darley Arabian	Byerley "Turk"	Leedes Arabian	Darcy White "Turk"	Darcy Yellow "Turk"	Lister "Turk"	Helmsley "Turk"	Old Bald Peg Arabian Mare	Sultan Arabian
Big Game	28232	44079	64032	187197	90420	294508	63832	109946	367162	367162
Sun Chariot	42079	68394	94706	169899	230307	279293	60717	102912	233579	233579
Hyperion	15594	23998	32199	31426	118182	111938	22350	41003	138827	138827
Fairway	14931	22734	33188	58350	50252	92804	18662	34478	113740	113740
Windsor Lad	25376	38944	61783	93573	103753	152544	30366	56880	184091	184091

This table shows the number of repeat crosses of some foundation sires of our classic winners showing also the repeat crosses of the Arabian Mare "Old Bald Peg." "Turk" was an alternative term for an Arabian and was often used for horses imported from Syria which was occupied by the Turks and for a time called Turkey.

Sun Chariot's direct sire line is the Darley Arabian and she belongs in direct female line to No. 3 Bruce Lowe family which traces back to the same as No. 2 (Burton Barb mare). Big Game is from the same sire line and he descends in female line from No. 6 the Arab mare 'Old Bald Peg' so not only is she his tap root mare but he has over quarter of a million repeat crosses of her blood.

It is difficult for the public to realize the full magnificence of classic thoroughbred conformation as the horses they see on race-courses are mostly immature youngsters in hard training, numbers of which look weedy, ewe-necked and high on the leg. There is nothing finer than the highest type of classic stallion in full maturity. The ideal thoroughbred should have a small alert head with straight or slightly concave profile, large eye, broad forehead, elegant throttle, small sharply cut mobile ears; long, nicely curved neck (strongly crested in stallions); deep chest; long shoulder with high withers well laid back; elbows free and forelegs set well forward; back of medium length with immensely strong loins and level quarters with tail well set on and often well carried. The quarters and thighs cannot be too long and powerful and muscular as this is where the propelling force comes from; there is an extremely straight drop of hind leg; joints are apt to be rather small and cannon bones too long, but these are defects; great bone is not required so long as the tendons are strong and straight and well defined. A thoroughbred should have all the best points of a technically good horse with an added look of quality and aristocratic blood. He should stride out well at a walk—the hind feet well overstepping the track of the forefeet, but his action trotting is not high; galloping he should stretch out with immense freedom of shoulder action with a smooth sweeping stride, covering the ground with consummate ease and bringing his stifles well forward with a powerful swing something like a greyhound. Up and down or rounded action, jerkiness or clumsiness, detract from speed as also does a habit of changing perpetually from one leading leg to another or star gazing and flinging

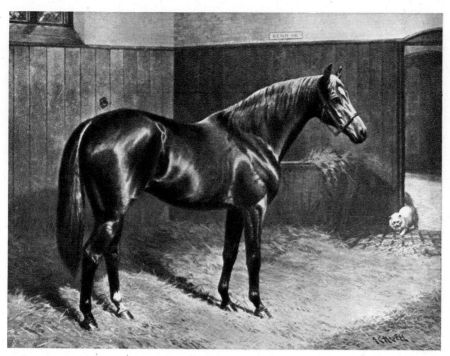

"BEND OR"
From the painting by A. C. Havell

the head about. Gliding and swinging, best describes the proper galloping movement. It is a mistake to think that a goose rump or drooping quarters are good points. The best sires are long but very level behind and the hips filled up with muscle. In height they range from 15.2 to 17 hands.

Thoroughbreds are of sensitive highly strung temperament, and rough usage quickly spoils their tempers. Early racing during teething time makes them inclined to fractiousness and irritability but they are naturally of friendly disposition and amenable to good horsemanship. The greatest miracle of the age which puts Britain in the highest rank of horsebreeders is the modern thoroughbred speed. It reached its climax when Mahmoud won the Derby in 1936 in the record time of 2 mins. $33\frac{3}{5}$ secs. Hyperion and Windsor Lad had previously held it with 2.34. Man o' War beat the lot with $2.28\frac{1}{5}$ and Pharlap with 2.29 over $1\frac{1}{2}$ miles, but not on the Derby course. Speed has been steadily increasing and nothing else in the world can compete with it. Unfortunately, but perhaps naturally, stamina has decreased equally rapidly and the old four mile heats are never run at all. It is doubtful whether extreme sprinting speed can be combined with extreme staying power as they are possibly antagonistic powers. A weight lifter is not built like an acrobat and a conformation which specializes one thing may be harmful to another. Soundness is becoming a serious problem.

Laminitis, split pasterns, unsound hocks, sprained tendons, bad tempers and increasing barrenness are some of the evils which attend premature racing and which may go on getting worse.

Meanwhile we have some horses to be proud of. Hyperion has proved that a small horse may not only beat records in speed but also records as a sire of winners. He and Mahmoud have made hay of the racing prejudice against horses with four white feet and greys. We owe the preservation of the grey colour to France through Le Sancy and Roi Hérode, from which we got the transcendant wonder-horse The Tetrarch, Tetratema, Mahmoud, the flying Mumtaz Mahal and other grey winners all going back to the White Alcock Arabian.

Prices are rapidly increasing to a staggering degree. The top price for brood mares being 17,000 guineas and the top prices for stallions, 40,000 to 62,000 guineas. Well bred yearlings may fetch anything from 2,000 to 14,000 guineas.

THE ANCIENT THOROUGHBRED "KEHILAN" RACING ARABIAN FOUNDATION BREED. The hot-blooded Arabian breed which has revolutionised our horse stock is indigenous to Arabia, once a fertile land of forests and rivers before the volcanic period of destruction and increasing drought. Originally wild, the breed is distinguished by characteristics marking it as a separate species ; and it has been preserved in Arabia from all foreign admixture. It has, normally, 5 lumbar vertebrae instead of 6, and generally 17 pairs of ribs instead of the 19 of the common horse and 18 of the Thoroughbred. This count of ribs is mentioned in the Indian sacrificial rites and in old Arabic veterinary mss., and it has been verified at the Crabbet Stud. Arabians are known by many named strains but all are of the same "Kehilan" (thoroughbred) stock. All strains should have the same pure type and be equally good, for though individual breeders may achieve celebrity no one strain is intrinsically better than another and the story of "El khamsa," the five mares of the Prophet, is just a romantic fiction.

Arabian horses have been imported to this country from the earliest records of their history and have been regularly bred here for the last 400 years and have appeared in the G.S.B. and earlier stud books since the seventeenth century. The imported stallions and mares (notably the Royal Mares of Charles II) have become famous as foundations of the Thoroughbred racehorse. In the nineteenth century some systematic importations of mares were made by the Blunts and others at the suggestion of Mr. Weatherby who reserved a special section for them in the G.S.B. thus reviving a traditional custom which had fallen into disuse.

CHARLES II's ROYAL MARE
Oil painting by J. Sartorius, Senior, c. 1685

THE HUNTER AND THE HACK: A TYPICAL COB
Oil painting by John Ferneley, 1782-1860

The Crabbet Park Stud has since become famous and has exported large numbers of improved Arabians to all parts of the globe, especially U.S.A., Russia, Australia, Egypt and Spain. The standard has been raised by selection and good feeding beyond anything that can now be produced in Arabia where climatic and other conditions tend to deterioration in size and numbers to an alarming degree. The Arab is now part of our British collection of breeds and those bred in England for generations though not specialized for speed are found to be so much faster than they are in their own country that Crabbet Stock has been barred from racing abroad unless running under the same weights as Thoroughbreds. This, though complimentary, is not quite fair as they cannot be expected to keep pace with Thoroughbreds. In sprinting speed they are outclassed and the only sphere in which they have met and defeated Thoroughbreds in open competition has been in the American races where Arabs have shown so great a superiority that not a single Thoroughbred could finish the course even when raced under easier conditions.

The Arabian is still the fastest natural breed not artificially specialised for speed, and still ranks next to his improved descendant the Thoroughbred racehorse ; and it is only in the last fifty years that English racing times have far outpaced the Arab times. No other horse can now approach the Thoroughbred for speed, but the Arab is the only one whose progeny of late years won races on the British Turf against Thoroughbreds ; and none can approach the Arab for stamina. The world records for long distance racing open to all breeds including Thoroughbreds are held by Arabs. A horse called Crabbet won over a 310 mile course of record severity carrying $17\frac{1}{2}$ stone in addition to several other races over 100 miles ; and a mare Ramla won over the same distance carrying $14\frac{1}{2}$ stone followed by a mile race next day. He is a good riding and light harness horse with an affectionate and friendly temper and fond of human companionship. His intelligence is remarkably developed and he is so easily teachable that he is the most popular subject for High School and circus tricks. He has a peculiar facility for turning figures of eight in a small space without breaking step, and this makes him a delightful and handy hack. He is also a good jumper and will clear four feet of timber in the hunting field, but is inclined to be hot with hounds, so for hunting an Anglo-Arab cross will be found ideal—a bit bigger and a bit steadier than the pure Arab and with bigger stride to negotiate heavy plough.

A true Arab should be full of fire and vitality. A ewe-necked, weedy, lifeless stallion is not worth his keep, and stallions which look like mares should be avoided as sires. A sire should have a strong, arched crest and a flashing eye and be of a bold though good tempered disposition. Mares are quieter but should also be showy and striking to look at.

The points of the Arab horse are : head small and profile concave, tapering to a very small muzzle ; eyes very large and brilliant and circular, and placed much lower in the skull than the eyes of other horses; forehead extremely broad; nostrils very flexible and set on in line with the profile (not at the end of the nose) and capable of enormous expansion; jowl very deep and wide, and the bars of the mouth much longer than in ordinary horses; ears small and very sharply cut, quick and pricked; neck arched and set in to the jaws in an arched curve, the windpipe being extra detached and loose; the withers are not so high as to be "ox-shouldered" but slope into a strong level back; they may be broader than those of other horses; chest broad and deep; body well ribbed up; quarters broad and level; tail set on a level with the back and carried high; legs with iron tendons, large strong hocks, big flat knees, springy pasterns and well developed thighs; feet hard and round; action free and fast both at trot and walk. Imported Arabs seldom exceed 14.3; those bred in England have reached over 16 hands. Of late years good Arabs have fetched prices from 2,000 to 6,000 guineas and far higher prices have been refused including £45,000 for the famous champion Skowronek.

MIXED LIGHT BREEDS

Post Horses, Coach Horses and Hunters of the Eighteenth and Early Nineteenth Centuries. All our roadsters are descended from these and have diverged from them owing to heavier crosses at different periods which it is impossible to verify exactly. The types have coarsened considerably and are heavier in bone and have much less quality in practically every case. These early hunters and carriage horses were of the same oriental origin as the racehorse as can be seen in the beautiful aquatints of that period. They had small and beautiful heads, arched necks and high tail carriage and were brilliant movers. Artists emphasized this in giving a vivid reproduction of what they saw. Our ancestors were always writing about the "game cock throttle," the arch of the throat, which means so much both in free wind power and beauty, but which many of us seem to have almost forgotten. We know that the post and coach horses had to do astonishing distances at a gallop pulling heavy weights in all weathers and over very heavy roads.

Trotting horses have been known as far back as Roman times. During the nineteenth century the trotters were not considered a distinct breed but the result of careful selective crosses of racing blood, and Sidney states that originally they had "beautiful heads like Arabs," though in his day (late nineteenth century) they were extraordinarily coarse, everything being sacrificed to action. The favourite colours were silver roan, red roan, bay brown and chestnut, with as few white markings as possible. Eight and a half inches below the knee was considered a good measurement. This betrays cart blood.

A TANDEM
Coloured engraving after H. Alken

NORFOLK TROTTERS are believed to be of Scandinavian extraction but Old Shields (alias Shales) was by Blank out of a hunter mare. In the last century they were about 15.2, and resembled a refined Suffolk Punch or a Clydesdale. They had extravagant action over short distances but were then getting too heavy for long fast journeys. Marshland Shales (1802) was called a "thundering trotter" and could go at twenty miles an hour but his knee action was not very high. It is difficult to guess exactly where the abnormally high action originated unless it was from the same source as the Chinese high steppers.

YORKSHIRE COACH HORSES descend from the same famous sires as the trotters and came originally from both Norfolk and Lincolnshire. It is evident that the Yorkshire Coach horse and the Cleveland Coach horse had many ancestors in common and were largely interbred though the Clevelands had a substratum of heavier blood. The origin of the two former breeds was almost identical for a hundred years ; their character-

27

istics were due mainly to Spanish Hackney blood of the type imported by the Duke of Buckingham with gilt saddles and trappings ; they were fast trotters and showy horses and the Yorkshire trotters could carry heavy weight. Dreadnought trotted 16 miles in an hour carrying 16 stone and Plato went 18 miles carrying 18 stone in the same time ; while King William did a mile in 3 minutes under 14 stone. A team of Coach horses, in 1750, drew a carriage and 4 postillions, totalling 3 tons 4 cwt., 19 miles in 53 minutes 27 seconds.

HACKNEYS.

> *"Prince of Palfreys who trots the air and makes the earth sing as he touches it with his elastic tread."*
>
> *Richard III*

This breed is descended from the celebrated trotting roadsters of the eighteenth century, which were of the same root stock as the hunters but with a stronger infusion of Spanish Andalusian blood on which much Arab blood (Darley and Godolphin Arabian and Flying Childers) was superimposed (Trotting Jalap was by Regulus). Like all fiery, 'quality' horses, oriental blood is the source of their vital spark. The word "hack" meant originally a riding horse, and in 1298, at the Battle of Falkirk a "Hackney" value 8 marks was killed so they seem also to have been used for light cavalry.

There was a constant influx of Spanish harness horses into this country for centuries, as many as fifty Andalusians being imported as long ago as

MODERN HACKNEY TEAM
Judge Moore and his famous Team of Bays

28

BRIGHTON COACH
Nineteenth century coloured aquatint by W. J. Sayers

Edward III's reign, and this Spanish ancestry of the Hackneys provides us with a possible link with ancient China. For in early Chinese art of the fifteenth century B.C. we find extravagantly high-stepping horses which are almost identical with the hackney type of to-day, and as China was chiefly remarkable for the coarseness of its ancient breeds (which were of Mongolian ugliness) it appears possible that Spanish traders may have exported Spanish horses.

In 1729 an Arab stallion 15.3 and a Yorkshire stallion were sent to cover in Norfolk and the breeds were much intermingled. Turning to modern times we find that a horse called Old Shales (alias Shields) is one of the foundation sires in the Hackney Stud Book. He was grandson of Flying Childers out of a hunter mare, which was possibly Spanish as were a number of hunters at that time.

Reads Fireaway in 1801 trotted 1 mile in 2 minutes 49 seconds and the same day 16 miles in 58 minutes, carrying 16 stone. In 1820 a horse trotted 100 miles in 11 consecutive hours on the Ipswich Road, carrying 12 stone for the first 50 miles, and 7 stone for the second. In 1822 Wood-cock's blind mare covered 40 miles on the London Road in 3 hours 43 minutes, and Dyson's Wonder went 3 miles in 8 minutes 43 seconds carrying 15 stone 4 lbs. In 1832 Non Pareil was driven 100 miles in 9 hours 56 minutes 57 seconds. These ancestors of the Hackney had lots of stamina.

The chief points are : head small, convex, tapering to the muzzle; eyes large ; ears small ; neck rather long and thick set ; shoulders good but usually low in withers. The formlessness of the withers, which show no dip where the top line of the neck joins them, is characteristic but does not interfere with their action : girth and middle piece inclined to be shallow and tightly modelled ; tail set on and carried high ; legs short and hocks strong ; feet good ; colour mostly dark brown and black, and four white feet are common in the best strains and used to be much liked —this again is a link with Spain ; height from 14.3 to 15.3 sometimes reaching 16.2. Coat silky. The shoulder action is exceedingly free, the knee action high but must not consist of an up-and-down, perpendicular stamping. The foreleg must be thrown right forward, the foot dwelling a moment in the air before it reaches the ground with that peculiar grace which makes a horse seem to float and fly over the ground. The hock action must be free, the stifle joint being well brought forward. There should be no dishing or side to side throwing. Freedom of movement and stride are essential.

HACKNEY PONIES which are a smaller edition of the breed, are among the handsomest of harness ponies and go a great pace with delightful ease and freedom. Their height may be up to 14 hands. There are many good Hackney Studs and Hackneys have been exported extensively and are the chief source of the magnificent American saddle horses crossed with Arabs. Since the decline of harness work in England they are essentially spectacular show ring horses though a few teams were still running in the last remaining four-in-hand coaches which survived the motor traffic before the war.

CAVALRY AND POLICE HORSES. The world's best cavalry horses were bred in Poland, Italy and Hungary and had a very large proportion of Arab blood. There was a careful system of breeding also in France with Arab, Thoroughbred, Lippizza and Native blood. Some magnificent hunters could be seen in Italy. The system is given in my book *The Authentic Arabian Horse*. The success of the Austrian and Italian Cavalrymen in jumping classes at all the International Shows is well known and the system of breeding and training might well be followed in England for breeding hunters now that cavalry regiments have been mechanized. A magnificent police horse was billeted here in 1941. He was bred from "a Crabbet Arab" and was 17.2 hands and very powerful and handsome. One type of Police horse looks as if it had been bred much the same way as the Continental Cavalry chargers. The ones for gun teams were more coarsely bred at German Studs regardless of looks for Germany has never gone in

TRAINING FOR CIRCUS WORK

for beauty of any kind. At one time they specialized in breeding freaks and managed to produce horses with extravagantly long manes and tails and strange spots and streaks. Professor Littmann however wrote an interesting treatise on the ancient Oldenburg horse which had oceans of wavy mane and tail and was also a magnificent creature of the High School type. This is now represented best in the Hungarian White Lippizza.

POLO PONIES are not a breed but a mixture of many breeds, Arabs, Thoroughbreds and Crossbreeds. The raising of the height limit from 14.2 has been a doubtful blessing as it admits a heavier type of pony which knocks out the lighter type and increases the cost of the game, making it a game for the few richer men, who can afford a long price, instead of a game within reach of the many who cannot. It is in fact becoming semi-professionalized being more of a serious business than the sport it used to be. Before this alteration Arab polo ponies were pre-eminent for their cleverness, quickness and miraculous turning powers, just as they are pre-eminent in India for pig sticking, but now they have been ridden off the field by the sheer weight of the bigger ponies and with them go many young polo players whose purses cannot compete with the increased expenses.

It is a pity there cannot be two recognised grades of game, a 14.2 limit and an over 14.2 open game. In 1891 Mr. Hill purchased several very typical Welsh pony mares of 10 hands and put them to an Arab producing handsome 13 hand stock which was re-crossed to a 14.2 Welsh stallion and progressively to thoroughbred sires producing excellent Polo ponies. It would appear now that the best cross would be a varying admixture of Anglo-Arab with a dash of Welsh if required, should the height reach the hunter class and become over tall even for the present game.

PARADE HORSES

THE WHITE PROCESSIONAL BREED. The magnificent white horses still used in the Royal processions are among the finest in the world and seem to be a compound of the lovely Lippizza High School horse (shown at Olympia a few years ago) and the ancient Oldenburg type. These horses are well worth preserving and are very large and strong and could well improve our agricultural breeds. H.M. King George has some remarkably fine mares which should be bred from before it is too late to save them from extinction. I believe they were bred in Holland.

THE CREAM BREED. Queen Victoria made these famous as her special carriage horses and though they used to be called "the Cream Ponies" they were really nearly 16 hands and very handsome. They were bred

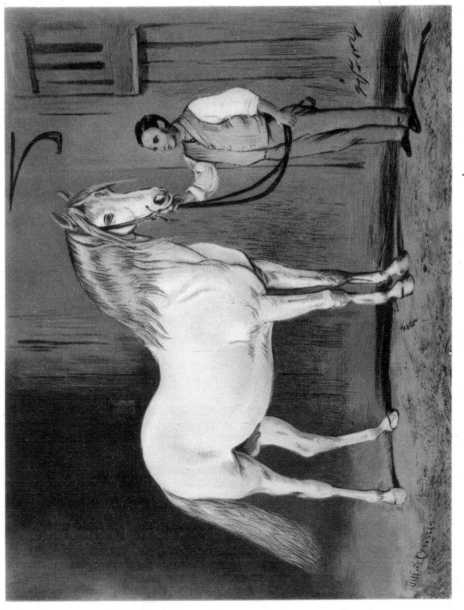

CREAM STATE CARRIAGE HORSE OF QUEEN VICTORIA'S STUD
Coloured lithograph after Alfred Corbould
From Sidney's *Book of the Horse*, 1875

HYDE PARK CORNER

Coloured engraving after J. Pollard, 1797 - c.1859

in Hanover and have almost died out in England as the Stud was recently dispersed much to public regret as they added greatly to Royal pageantry.

THE BLACK BREED of Funeral Horses were Hanoverian but are gradually becoming scarce and less well bred owing to the use of motor hearses. The true breed bore a strongly Spanish appearance with high arched crests and sweeping curly manes and tails. They were intense blue-black stately horses, slow and picturesque, and quite an asset to the pomp of a funeral. There was a large breed of black coach horses in Lincolnshire in the sixteenth century which was probably of similar origin as they were essentially carriage horses with a rather slow high trot in front but not much hind action. This was not the same as the Dutch cart breed imported by William III.

CIRCUS HORSES. The type of circus horse familiar to the Public is of foreign origin, Eastern horses being the most spectacular and odd coloured "Apeloosas" (Apeloosas are white horses speckled with black like leopards) and other speckled and piebald breeds being much in demand. Though bred abroad they are and have been for many years trained for circus work solely in England and I must here emphasize that there is no cruelty training horses or dogs in this country. Animals which have been ill-treated always betray it in an unwilling or timid performance. Our English Circus horses and dogs clearly enjoy their own tricks and are eager to earn applause and they are never allowed to do dangerous tricks. Teachers of course vary in their capacity for animal control. The best are obeyed without effort or question. Horses must be kept in tip top condition if only for the sake of the show. A thin animal is not spectacular and the Shetlands always prance into the ring as fat as dormice drawing Cinderella's coach. Whips may crack ever so fiercely but to the horses they are a signal not a threat.

Pure white horses probably are bred in Lippizza where there have been big studs which were famous for their "High School" riding horses of Spanish-Arab-Barb descent. These are trained in Vienna and were seen at the fine display at Olympia some years ago. They are not, properly speaking, circus horses but, of course, very adaptable. Great intelligence is needed for circus work combined with good temper, fire and suppleness, especially in the Liberty stallions which dance on their hind legs and perform intricate evolutions at liberty without riders in batches of assorted colours. In America they still have the dangerous performance of jumping off a high diving board into a water tank, but in England this is not allowed. For acrobatic turns a broad backed horse of placid temperament is essential ; a horse which can be trusted to canter slowly and steadily, without breaking step, of its own accord round the ring while the acrobats leap on and off its back, make pyramids, stand on their heads and turn somersaults.

ANGLO-ARABS. As long ago as 1822 Charles Davis, huntsman of the Goodwood foxhounds, a 10 stone man, described as the finest horseman and most fastidious horsemaster of his century, rode as his best hunter a grey Anglo-Arab by the thoroughbred horse Grey Isaac out of a white Arab mare imported from Egypt. The pioneer of the breed to-day is Lady Yule who breeds extraordinarily fine strong horses from 15.3 to 16.3 with a longer front and higher withers and longer stride than the pure Arab and with stronger quarters, more level back, sounder limbs, feet and wind and a better temper than the thoroughbred. They are in fact the ideal hunter and hack, fine bold jumpers with a great turn of speed. They have the courage and generosity of the Arab and the size and greater scope of the racehorse.

The cross from T.B. Stallion and Arab mare or vice versa with their subsequent re-crossing are what are technically termed and registered as Anglo-Arabs, but part-bred Arab crosses and ponies of all sizes and for all purposes can be produced by suitably selected Arab Crosses on almost every breed of mare including Welsh ponies, and are also now eligible for registration in the part bred section of the Anglo-Arab stud book. The smaller ones are also eligible for the National Pony stud books. An Arab cross with Percheron or other well bred agricultural mares gives an extra heavy-weight hunter or harness horse. The Anglo-Arab is the only breed which has been able to make any show whatever against Thoroughbreds in recent times on the English Turf. In the last century Lilias (Anglo-Arab) won the Oaks and another Anglo-Arab, a grey horse called Exhibitionist, was second in the Derby while in the last few decades horses bred from Crabbet Stock in England have won 54 races on the English Turf. A gelding called Chip won no less than 22 races often giving top weight, once winning by distance. He was second 19 times and third 12 times. Alfragan by Chippendale out of a half Arab mare won the Dee Stakes and the Drayton High Weight Handicap and grandsons and granddaughters of an Arab mare Debora won many races.

HACKS may be bred in the same way as hunters. A hack should have a good wither to keep the saddle back and a long flexible neck, a good mouth and manners. A puller is a nuisance. He should not have too high knee action or you will get a shaking. A slow cantering action, very smooth and under control, is essential ; a free but not extravagant trot, a fast free walk and easy gallop : the walk must be cultivated and developed, as fast and steady walking at full stretch is not really a horse's natural pace any more than long sustained trotting at high speed. Slow cantering and quick turning with an easy smooth change of leg are a necessary asset and hacks should be taught to start into a canter from a standstill, or walking

"Le Ra"
Lady Yule's Champion Anglo-Arab Hunter

pace without trotting first. A horse being turned at a canter must on no account be allowed to "break" (*i.e.*, drop into a hop-trot) when changing his direction ; this is an awkward habit too often seen even in the show ring. No hack should have jerky movements ; he should move rhythmically, and when he jumps he should glide over his fences like a swallow, not jerk over them like a tiddley-winks counter. He should be trained to be handy when you are opening gates and not back away from them or rush suddenly through and jam your knee on the post.

It is a pity that amblers should have so completely gone out of fashion, as for sheer comfort and quick travelling the pace is delightful ; one can carry a glass brimful of water without spilling it as they speed along. I am not here speaking of the American racing pace but the old riding amble sometimes still found in Egypt and the East.

A hack should be taught to stand still when mounted and should never start off the moment a foot is put in the stirrup. He should also stand still if the rider gets off ; nothing looks more absurd than being obliged to hop on one foot after a horse, and scrambling into the saddle anyhow. No

35

hack should kick and still less rear or jib ; it is quite useless putting up with these faults, unless you enjoy a stand up fight as there are "plenty more fish in the sea." A kicker may break another rider's ankle if he comes too close to you. A rearer may fall back on you and break your pelvis and a serious jibber makes a fool of you, so unless you are out horse-breaking give them all a miss.

COBS. Any sturdy thick set, broad backed horse up to about 15 hands and 14 stone is popularly termed a cob, and may be of any mixture of blood containing a proportion of cart ancestry crossed with pony blood and probably some Hackney and pack horse. They have a certain type of their own well shown in the well-known picture by Ferneley. They stand on short legs with much bone for their size and are thick all through and are a strong and useful cross breed.

WELSH COBS. Founded on the same Celtic and Arab stock as the smaller ponies ; they diverged later on in Cardiganshire and Breconshire owing to Norfolk Trotter and Hackney sires. This produced high action but increased height to cob size and coarsened the type. They are a commercially useful type for farmers and tradesmen being good roadsters and able to pull and carry weight. Of late years they have been much further coarsened by Cart-Hackney crosses and are getting clumsy compared to the better type still found in S. Wales and which contains a large proportion of eastern blood. A very good type was bred from Lord Penrhyns Caradoc by Caractacus (Derby winner) with Welsh mares in the Merioneth district.

It will be seen that cobs may be bred in various ways ; "Cob" is really a term for a stocky thick strong general utility horse about 13.2 to 14.2 and refers to size and build more than breed. The term Galloway was the Scotch equivalent for a somewhat faster type.

HUNTERS of the eighteenth century were of strongly Arab type and not very different to the galloping coach and post horses of the period. They were a very beautiful, quality type, small headed, light limbed, and much like the Thoroughbred racehorse of that time. Some had an admixture of Spanish blood but show little trace of it by 1823. Both had to be free movers and capable of doing long distances. Hobby horses were horses used for hawking and coursing and the Irish hobbies were often pacers. They are now a mixture of all sorts. A hunter should be an active strong horse from 15.2 to 16.2 and may be of any breed or mixture of breeds that is well shaped, of good temperament, fast, long winded and of enduring constitution and sound limbs and feet. Great ponderousness should be avoided. Activity is far more important than avoirdupois and too heavy a horse is often awkward at turning in woodland rides, and if he comes down over a fence is likely to lie on his rider for an unpleasant time to get back his wind, where a lighter horse will be on its feet immediately ! A heavy-weight hunter need not have legs like a kitchen table. It is the quality

THE MASTER OF HOUNDS, LORD GLAMIS
Engraving by S. W. Reynolds after D. Wolstenholme, 1825

and flatness of bone, not its measurement, which carry weight. The world's leading champion weight carriers are horses with short backs and iron tendons but are not remarkable for size below the knee.

Modern hunters tend to be far too clumsy, heavy boned and big footed and a leading veterinary authority tells me they are "always in trouble" one way or another. These awkward animals with their heavy heads and hard mouths are rough rides not to speak of being extremely unpleasing to the eye. The ideal hunter is an Anglo-Arab either half and half or three-quarters bred. There is nothing to equal this though heavier horses may be bred from an Arab-Percheron cross.

IRISH HORSES. The Limestone pastures of the South Midland and Western Counties have a high reputation, and the hunters bred on them have long been outstanding. "Hobby," *i.e.*, hawking horses and Irish pacers appear in the earliest horse history and the Saga of Cuchulain gives a dramatic description of swift harness horses. The original stock was of much the same origin as that of England and we find the same history of Spanish, Arab and Barb importations from the early seventeenth century onwards. Races were instituted in 1673 by Sir W. Temple and later the Byerley Turk stood in Ireland as a stallion. In 1833 Barb and Arab sires were sent to the West of Ireland by Col. Martin and 100 years earlier Morocco mares were landed at Cork. Othello by Crab (Alcock Arabian) also served in Ireland. There was a very fine breed of old farm horse, too heavy for hunting but with a natural aptitude for jumping and these draught mares mated to Thoroughbreds later produced the present type of Irish hunter famous all over the world. Taken as a whole they are of uniform type with great strength and massive quarters and much bone and the type of draught mare from which they descend is a short backed, short legged, powerful animal with a slightly convex head and great endurance. A stud book was started for them in 1917.

Irish breeders have specialized in jumping and the Irish jockeys and Irish steeplechasers hold a remarkable record. From 1900 to 1936 Irish bred horses have won the Grand National 25 times. Golden Miller and Reynoldston were Irish bred and the English National Stud when established in Ireland made history on the flat with Big Game, Sun Chariot and Windsor Slipper, but the hunter type is more particularly Irish being founded on Native Irish mares. Irishmen are born horsemen and judges of horses. The soft Irish brogue seems to delight the equine race. Horses like being talked to and even sung to when they are being groomed. Irishmen have a natural "way" with horses and a mixture of blarney and firmness, an intuition and sympathy which makes them the best of breakers and riders from the unknown farm boy to the great Steve Donoghue whose genius won him the heart of the whole British public, with a record of six Derbys including a "hat trick" of three in succession.

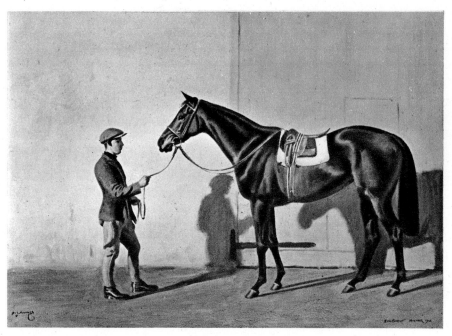

"SUN CHARIOT"
Oil painting by A. J. Munnings

PONIES

All our pony breeds are Celtic in origin crossed with various proportions of oriental blood. The Shetland alone seems to be an original prehistoric species of its own.

SHETLAND PONIES. These belong to the Shetland Isles but are widely distributed all over Britain and even on the continent ponies of this type can be found. They are not only exceedingly pretty but the world's smallest breed, being the only breed which sometimes is only 24 inches high without deformity. In spite of their toy-like size they are so strong that the larger ones have been extensively used as pit ponies. No more fascinating mount for children could be imagined and they have been universally popular as such for centuries both for riding and driving. They can trot a great pace for their size. Mr. Lacy's Beauty, a $10\frac{1}{2}$ hand Skewbald mare, trotted 10 miles in $39\frac{1}{2}$ minutes driven by a man weighing 11 st. 4 lbs. She also did a mile in 3 min. 44 sec., and 14 miles in 55 min. 45 sec. Shetlands live to a great age, often to 30 years, and one called

Topsy is recorded to have lived to be 44. They are said to be immune from strangles which is unknown in the Shetland Isles. The Stud book was started in 1889 and Lady Estella Hope has a very large Stud of the ponies—large in numbers but exceedingly small in size, some being only two feet high.

Their points are : heavy coat in winter, satin smooth in summer ; height under 10½ hands ; very short backed solid and compact, short legged with good feet and legs ; very small and pretty head of Arab character, broad forehead, very large, bright eyes and large flexible nostrils ; small muzzle, wide jaw, very small ears ; neck strong but not short and with a nice crest ; level quarters and tail set on a level with the back, extremely profuse mane, tail and forelock ; action very quick and brisk ; hocks well flexed and feet thrown well forward with very free shoulder action. Disproportionately big heads are a sign of common blood or of early starvation and arrested body growth. These ponies should be full of life and bounce, pleasantly wilful but good tempered. Sluggishness, coarseness, thick big ears and small eyes are a sign of some inferior cross. Colours are now, owing to fashion, chiefly dark bay, brown or black, but in my opinion skewbald and piebald are prehistoric original colours and should be preserved and encouraged. They generally accompany good conformation. Grey is now rare but should not be allowed to die out.

ICELAND PONIES, are much like large Shetlands and may be the origin of some of our pony types. The good ones are most attractive and well bred in appearance and exceedingly strong and useful. They have small heads and ears, and profuse manes and tails which latter are set high on a level back. Their eyes are large and they move well.

NORWEGIAN PONIES have been also used for crossing and their typical dun colour and black dorsal and shoulder stripes sometimes appear in the Welsh and Highland stock. They are handsome and very sturdy and are believed to have had a cross of Arab like most of the Celtic types. There are small and large ones, the small ones showing the best type. Very handsome with arched necks and crests, small heads and ears, a level back and well set, well carried tails.

HIGHLAND PONIES. These are very pretty ponies round about 12 to 13 hands. There is a larger size called Garron which ranges about 14.2 but it is not looked on with favour by the Highland Society as it has been crossed with cart horse. This mainland type is descended from the Western Isles pony, a sharp, alert, thick set, strong animal for carrying loads, riding, driving and light farm work.

The superior Highland ponies have been standardized to the following type: Head well carried and attractive, and broad between eyes; prominent

FOX HUNTING

Coloured acquatint by R. G. Reeve after D. Wolstenholme, 1806

COURSING: ONE OF THE OLDEST BRITISH SPORTS
Coloured acquatint by J. Pollard after S. N. Sartorius

bright and kindly eyes ; short between eyes and muzzle with wide nostrils ; ears short and well set. Viewed in profile the breadth rather than the length of the head and jawbone should be pronounced ; neck strong but not short ; crest arched with flowing mane ; throat clean, not fleshy ; shoulders well set back, withers not too pronounced ; body compact ; back short with slight natural curve, chest deep, ribs deep, well sprung and carried well back ; quarters and loins powerful and thighs short and strong ; tail strong and well set on and carried gaily, with a plentiful covering of hair almost reaching to the ground. Legs flat in bone, flinty to touch with a slight fringe of silken feathers in winter, but this must not amount to hairiness ; action free and straight ; colour—black, brown, fox colour with silver mane and tail, various shades of dun or grey with no white markings ; the eel stripe along back is a typical though not invariable feature denoting affinity with the Norwegian. They are hardy, sound, very useful and surefooted, and are probably allied to the Norwegian.

MIXED IMPROVED PONY BREEDS

New Forest. This is a crossbred of uncertain lineage which has been taken in hand and transformed of late years. In the middle ages all the New Forest, Dartmoor and Exmoor ponies were of debased type running wild in the woods and on the moors completely neglected and at the mercy of any scrub stallion anybody let loose. Though very hardy and strong it is only in the last centuries that some control has been exercised over the breeding. Thirty years ago Dr. Watney effected a great improvement by turning out a Crabbet Arab Stallion called Nejran, which by the way was the sire of a mare which cleared 32 feet over water out hunting. The type now aimed at is a 12.2 to 13 hand pony with free action and as well shaped as can be found but they vary very much with the amount of thoroughbred and Arab blood in them. Some are very nice looking with small heads and a look of breeding which their sponsors are successfully trying to fix but at present they cannot be called a type recognisable at sight among Dartmoor and Exmoor ponies similarly improved.

Exmoor Ponies are crossbred much in the same way as other Moorland ponies : the usual type is : height 11 hands to 12.2 ; black bay and dun with mealy noses—not chestnut ; dun points to a Norwegian cross ; clean cut and neat head, wide forehead, short, thick pointed ears ; short back, short shoulders, wide low withers, large nostrils and eyes ; quick and alert ; quarters wide but inclined to droop, and cow hocks are common but this does not prevent their carrying heavy weights. Exmoors were crossed at one time with Dongolese "Arabs" specially imported for the purpose but unsuitable as that breed is high on the leg and flat sided, with a rather convex head. It is black with blaze and very high white stockings and does not seem to have left much influence on the present ponies. In the eighteenth century a foreign stallion, Katerfelto, was running on Exmoor. The ponies are very active and good jumpers.

DARTMOOR. Another crossbred, 12.2, small, good head and ears, riding shoulders, tail well set, good bone and action ; all colours. A mixture of all sorts and an attractive harness and saddle pony.

DALES. Belong to Yorkshire and other northern counties. They are small active cart horses 14.2 or sometimes over. Black, brown bay, a few greys but variegated colours and chestnuts are never found in what is now called the pure breed. They have hair on the heels; quarters sloping; 8½ in. bone ; are good trotters and pack ponies.

FELL. The heaviest pony breed ; about 13.2. Belongs to the high Moorland and hill districts of the Northern Counties, probably descends from the Scotch Galloways and is still called Galloway. Thick and strong ; well set up tails ; heads not their best point ; 8 in. bone ; very powerful in harness and can carry heavy weights ; black or brown with few white markings ; also grey.

As the ponies were in danger of being obliterated by Clydesdale crosses a National Trust has just been founded in a deerpark of 7,550 acres on Gowbarrow Fell near Ullswater to preserve the right type of Fell pony from extinction. Mr. Summerhays tells us they used to work in droves of 20 carrying lead from the mines, 16 stone of lead slung pannierwise across their backs, 240 miles a week.

WELSH MOUNTAIN PONY. This is probably the most direct descendant of the small ponies of eastern origin shown on the early British coins. They were probably not originally confined to Wales but were driven to take refuge in the mountains of Wales and moorlands of Wales and Scotland to escape the wholesale pony massacre ordered by King Henry VIII. They all retain the Celtic type but Wales has specialized them during the last 3 centuries by repeated infusions of the best Arab blood and has now developed by in-breeding a most remarkable type of harness pony which is probably the world's best pony under 13 hands and is certainly the best looking. In the early eighteenth century the famous Arab bred T.B. Merlin was turned out on the hills. In 1842 the Earl of Oxford had a Welsh bred pony mare by the Clive Arabian, her dam also being by the Clive Arabian out of a Welsh pony mare which could beat any of his racehorses over 4 miles at a feather weight. This foundation blood accounts for the extreme beauty of some of the Welsh pony heads and the high carriage of their tails.

THE AUTHOR'S CHAMPION, "DEWDROP"
Typical Welsh Pony Mare of the "Starlight" Strain

THE GREY STARLIGHT STRAIN. At the beginning of this century a very
remarkable pony stamped his type on a large section of pony stock, being
very sensibly inbred over and over again has produced what in my opinion
is the world's best and most beautiful pony. Champion Dyoll Starlight is
said to have been sired by an unknown Arabian, and I have been told
on reliable authority that his dam was being taken for service to another
pony which for some reason was not available and the groom did not
report that she had been served instead by the Arab and hence it is not
recorded in the Welsh Stud Books.

It seems clear that the sire of Starlight must have been of outstanding
merit for he has stamped the breed with a class previously unknown. It
is of perfect proportions like a stout miniature Arab with marvellous spectacular action, a level back, high carried tail and lovely little head with
broad forehead and small ears, head tapering to the muzzle with wide open
fiery nostrils and enormous, brilliant eyes, a proudly carried arched neck,
the throttle set in a beautiful curve into a wide jaw ; sloped shoulders,
quarters wide and strong with model hocks and limbs and excellent feet.

43

"SKERRYVORE," HIGHLAND PONY STALLION

The usefulness of these ponies in harness cannot be exaggerated. Though under 12 hands (the regulation show limit) they are prodigiously strong and fast and trot along like the wind without tiring for long distances; they are sure footed and good tempered, and the strain should carefully be preserved. Indiscriminate Hackney and other crosses are undesirable as they produce convex heads and destroy the character of the breed, and it would be a pity to raise the height over 12.3. The larger ponies can be bred by those who like them but the small breed should be jealously preserved.

The Welsh Pony and Cob Society has divided the ponies into three classes: Welsh Mountain Pony up to 12 hands: Riding type ponies up to 13.2. The still larger cobs showing strong Hackney type, are good looking harness type; but high actioned cobs are generally rough rides and the higher the action the rougher the ride especially on a broad "cart-horsy" animal.

THE CONNEMARA PONY. This is a race long celebrated for hardiness, sureness of foot and general utility. Once again we find the ever recurring history of blood from Spain, Arabia and Morocco and probably the same

Phoenician "native" foundation. Until late years it retained the ambling pace of the Spanish Jennet. Unluckily the outlying districts have at times been disastrously contaminated by Clydesdale Stallions, Thoroughbreds, half breds and Hackneys. Welsh stallions have been successfully used. Cannon Ball some 20 years ago was a grandson of a Welsh Stallion Prince Llewellyn. In 1902 the breed was improved by Arab blood which infused quality.

Fifteen years ago a Society was formed to preserve what was considered the best type, i.e., a compact, deep bodied pony; short backed; well ribbed; standing on short legs with good bone; sloping shoulders and well balanced head and neck; height ranging from 13 to 14 hands and the best selected ponies about 13.2 with good action; bone 7 to 8 inches; (the old Spanish amble should in my opinion be encouraged in ponies of the Andalusian type as it is a hall mark of their ancestry); Colour grey, black, bay brown and dun with sometimes roan and chestnut; grey is the predominant colour; dun can be taken as a sign of Scandinavian Norwegian blood and as it was very prevalent before the indiscriminate crossing took place we may assume that there was much of the hardy Norseman's pony blood in the old stock. The prevalence of yellow ponies in the West of Ireland probably originates from the Palominos of N. Africa but where there are black points the Norwegian predominates.

CHILDREN'S PONIES may be found among any of the small breeds beginning with Shetlands. For young children between 5 and 9 a steady *old* pony is much best—young ponies cannot always be trusted, and ponies of 16 and 18 and even 20 years are not too old for the purpose, they are not as eager to prance and play up as the young ones. The chief points required are a good mouth, not too light but not hard, and a placid, good tempered disposition. Choose a pony with large kindly eyes and intelligent expression; a wither which by either height or breadth will keep the saddle in the middle of the back, good shoulder action and easy paces. Surefootedness is most important, so avoid marked knees. An old pony with clean knees is likely to be pretty certain on its legs or the knees would betray its past. Age does not appear to weaken the legs. Look out for turned-in toes or toes turned out, the pony should stand with its feet straight and should move straight. A great asset is a pony trained to stand still if the rider accidentally falls off, and wait about if the rider gets off on purpose.

A child's pony should not be too broad in the back so as not to stretch the rider's legs unduly but now that stirrups are worn so short this is not as important as it used to be and the most ideal child's pony of my acquaintance, Tan y Bwlch Gwyno, is by no means narrow; on the contrary she is like a miniature (elegant) cart horse but her manners are so perfect that no undue strain is put on the rider to keep in the saddle on her broad back.

AFTER THE WAR

As I have said the records of the British Isles for the last 2,000 years show a constant flow of importations, intercrossing, specialization and naturalization of foreign horses, for Britain depended entirely on foreign countries for all horse stock except possibly small pony breeds. Positions are now reversed and it is to England and Ireland that the whole world turns for its best horses—Britain holds the leading hand and practically all the trumps. It is England that has developed the world's greatest speed wonder the Racing Thoroughbred. Scotland initiated the largest and purest draught breed of the North. The Shetland Isles produces the smallest equine species, the delightful miniatures that look like toys. To Wales we owe the world's prettiest trotting ponies. Ireland, famed for its hunters, was the site of the National Stud. Even Arabia can produce no finer Arabians now than those bred here. We have just reason to be proud of all this.

We must, however, beware lest we lose our hardly won supremacy and allow the war and the free-handed and clever American breeders and other buyers to skim the cream from our stock.

In the last few years the rapidity of exodus among Derby winners has been alarming; the unbeaten Bahram, the record holder Mahmoud, Blenheim, Cameronian and, even worse, the Aga Khan's marvellous collection of mares, including the flying Mumtaz Mahal, and others. Where are they now? Where did these mares go? Nobody seems to know, but they are lost to us. We are left with a deplorably small lot of stud horses: Hyperion is there, but altogether inaccessible except to the favoured few. Fairway is almost equally out of reach, nominations being unobtainable. This is not for the benefit of the country. The same thing is happening with other breeds, Clydesdales have gone to U.S.A. en masse—the best Percherons have also been snapped up—some of the best Welsh ponies went to the U.S.A. and the marvellous Ch. Greylight to Australia and the World's Champion Arabs and some magnificent mares were secured by force of financial pressure for Russia, California and Spain. Much of this beautiful stock is lost or wasted but some of it may live to seriously challenge our supremacy.

The Government should support horse breeders and harass them as little as possible. At present the war has created havoc but if it teaches us to appreciate our horse stock once more this is a good thing. Thousands of people deprived of petrol and rubber have bought ponies and horses for transport and all the forgotten vehicles of every kind have been routed out of barns and sheds and refitted for the road. Perhaps some of the useful pony turnouts have come to stay—let us hope so, for, to a horse lover, entirely mechanised transport, and roads and fields without horses is a dismal prospect. When the time comes for remaking the roads consider-

PONIES

Exmoor Pony and Kiang Hybrid nine days old

"Cuach-na-Coille," Connemara Pony   "Stella," Arab-Welsh Child's Pony

"Black Bess," New Forest Pony   "The Leat," Dartmoor Stallion

ation should be given to providing a decent foothold for horses, the present steep cants and slippery surface being dangerous.

The future of hunting in England is likely to be restricted by the needs of agriculture but in Ireland we can hope that it will be as popular as ever. The Southern Counties of England have long been too cramped for hard riding. Huge areas of open country have been built over and covered with bungalows and allotments, and now vast tracts of meadowland have been reclaimed for ploughing, and if the country is to be self supporting in foodstuffs it will be impossible for the farming community of egg, milk and grain producers to have bands of horsemen galloping over their fields, nor would compensation suffice for the depredations of foxes and the breaking of fences, not to speak of the fact that a day's hunting over miles of plough and fields enclosed with barbed cattle wire, would damp the enthusiasm of the keenest M.F.H. and try the stamina of the stoutest horse. Hunters may therefore be less in demand and a lighter riding horse may well take its place.

The ancient feudal attitude of some English hunting communities belongs to an age of great landowners, and the hunting field has been threatened with an almost tyrannical code of sartorial despotism and etiquette which was fast turning a free sport into a dress parade. In no other athletic exercise do people truss themselves up in such tight, stiff clothes fit only for road riders and certainly not for serious work. It seems a relic of the old red coat army uniforms whose throttling collars, coats too tight under the arms and nether garments too tight to sit down, have had to be swept out of existence in serious warfare. In Ireland it is not dress that counts in the hunting field.

SHELTER ON FARMS. It is rather disturbing when we are told in authoritative circles that "all hedges must go" after the war and with them the ditches essential to land drainage. Whoever has watched cattle and horses crowding under trees and hedge-rows in summer time cannot but realize the vital necessity of hedgerow and tree protection, so that the ruthless sweeping away of these things would do more harm than good. It is just this sort of short-sighted one-idea ruling which is the despair of practical farmers and stock breeders whose activities include both growing and breeding and they should be nicely balanced and conducted so as not to damage each other. Huge tracts of unfenced country may be all right on paper but they are ugly to the last degree and it would be a pity to lose all sense of beauty in our anxiety to till the last yard of ground. Let us hope that we may still be allowed to preserve the lovely English scenery which has made the South of England famous.